HILLARY RODHAM CLINTON

Profile of a Leading Democrat

Jeri Freedman

ROSEN
PUBLISHING

To my niece and nephew, Laura and Matthew Freedman,
with love

Published in 2008 by The Rosen Publishing Group, Inc.

29 East 21st Street, New York, NY 10010

Copyright © 2008 by The Rosen Publishing Group, Inc.

First Edition

Library of Congress Cataloging-in-Publication Data

Freedman, Jeri.
Hillary Rodham Clinton: profile of a leading Democrat / Jeri Freedman. — 1st ed.
   p. cm. — (Career profiles)
Includes bibliographical references and index.
ISBN-13: 978-1-4042-1910-6
ISBN-10: 1-4042-1910-2
1. Clinton, Hillary Rodham—Juvenile literature. 2. Presidents' spouses—United States—Biography—Juvenile literature.
3. Legislators—United States—Biography—Juvenile literature.
4. Women legislators—United States—Biography—Juvenile literature.
5. United States. Congress. Senate—Biography—Juvenile literature.
I. Title.
E887.C55F74 2007
328.73092—dc22
[B]

2006039714

Manufactured in Malaysia

CONTENTS

INTRODUCTION

In many ways, the story of Hillary Rodham Clinton's life is the story of the later half of twentieth-century America and the generation of Americans who came of age at that time. Born in the post–World War II baby boom, she lived through the major events that changed and reshaped American society: the Cold War; the political activism of the 1960s; the assassinations of President John F. Kennedy, Martin Luther King, and Bobby Kennedy; the Vietnam War and its protests; the civil rights movement; and Watergate and the impeachment of President Richard M. Nixon.

Hillary marches in the 2000 St. Patrick's Day parade in New York City during her campaign for the U.S. Senate. Hillary is the only First Lady to hold an elected position.

During her tenure as First Lady, many people had strong feelings about Hillary—they either loved her or hated her. The controversy that has swirled around her reflects the controversy about the roles and rights of women in our society. Hillary Rodham Clinton has been a wife, mother, lawyer, children's advocate, First Lady of Arkansas, First Lady of the United States, and senator from New York. Despite her prominence, in many ways her experiences are typical of many women in the late twentieth and early twenty-first centuries. She has had to fill multiple, often conflicting, roles and has faced prejudice in the workplace. However, she has also had opportunities that were available to no previous generation of women.

Part of living through a period of changing expectations and roles is the way it changes you. The Democratic Party is often viewed as the more liberal of the two major American political parties. Democrats have traditionally favored social change and supported programs such as Social Security and welfare. Given Hillary's prominence in the Democratic Party and the efforts she has expended on issues such as health care and child welfare, you might expect that she was brought up to believe in the principles of the Democratic Party. Such is not the case, however. Hillary grew up in a conservative Chicago suburb in a Republican household, and her first political activities were with the Republican Party. This is the story of the events and experiences that led from Hillary's conservative beginnings to her position as a prominent Democrat.

ONE
GROWING UP IN THE POST-WAR YEARS

The years just after World War II (1939–1945) were a time of unbridled optimism in America. The war was over, and many people believed that it would be the last war in their lifetime. The damage done to the cities of Europe meant that they had to rely on American factories to supply the products they needed. Therefore, jobs were plentiful in America, and it seemed a great time to start a business and a family. Poor people and minorities still faced many hardships, but middle-class Americans were experiencing an unparalleled prosperity. They believed that this was the result of America's capitalist economy

Pictured here is Hillary as a small child in the early 1950s. Hillary grew up in the Chicago suburb of Park Ridge, Illinois.

(the generation of goods and services by private individuals and enterprises) and the pursuit of technology, as well as its predominantly white and Christian culture. They believed that they were living the best way, and they were determined to resist any change to their way of life. Into this atmosphere of social promise and political conservatism, Hillary Diane Rodham was born in Chicago on October 26, 1947.

Family History

Hillary's mother, Dorothy Howell, was of Welsh, Scottish, French-Canadian, and Native American ancestry. She was born on Chicago's South Side, a working-class neighborhood. Dorothy's mother (Hillary's grandmother), Della Murray, was only fifteen when Dorothy was born, and Dorothy's fireman father, Edwin John Howell Jr., was seventeen. When her parents got divorced, Dorothy was sent to live with her grandparents in California, where she spent most of her childhood. She graduated from high school in 1937. She had planned to go to college, but instead she returned to Chicago at the request of her long-estranged mother. While applying for a typist's job at the Columbia Lace Company, she met Hugh Rodham, a young drapery fabric salesman.

Hillary's father was of Welsh and English ancestry. He was born in Scranton, Pennsylvania, a city known for its mining, textile, and railroad industries. Hugh received a football scholarship to Pennsylvania State University and graduated with a degree in physical education. He entered the workforce during the Great Depression of the 1930s, when huge numbers of people were out of work. He did manual labor in a lace factory and worked in the Pennsylvania coal mines before finally landing a job as a salesman for a Chicago-based fabric company. He traveled around the Midwest selling drapery fabric. He was making a sales call on the company where Dorothy Howell was applying for work when they met. In 1942, shortly after the Japanese attack on Pearl Harbor, the couple married, and Hugh joined the navy. He trained sailors at the Great Lakes Naval Station north of Chicago during World War II.

Growing Up in Park Ridge

After the war, Hugh started his own drapery fabric business, doing much of his own fabric printing. Three years after Hillary's birth, the Rodhams had a second child, Hugh Jr. Shortly thereafter, the family moved to Park Ridge, Illinois, a suburb 15 miles (24 km) northwest of Chicago. Park Ridge was a charming town with tree-lined streets and excellent schools, where the Rodhams lived in a two-story brick house. It was there that Hillary's youngest brother, Tony, was born.

Life at Home

Like many of the suburbs of the time, Park Ridge was populated primarily by white middle-class people.

The Baby Boom

In the years following World War II, America experienced unprecedented prosperity, supplying goods to the world as European nations struggled to rebuild their bombed-out factories. Large numbers of men had returned home from war. These returning soldiers and sailors were able to attend college, using tuition benefits granted under the G.I. Bill, and college degrees allowed them to earn higher incomes. All of these factors led to a rapid increase in the number of couples having children in the years from 1945 to 1954. This phenomenon is often referred to as the baby boom, and those who were born during this period are called baby boomers. Baby boomers grew up during the Cold War between the United States and the Soviet Union, when the greatest political threats were perceived to be the spread of Communism and the potential for nuclear war between the two great superpowers. The baby boom generation participated in what is probably American's greatest period of social change—the 1960s and 1970s.

This is Hillary's childhood home in Park Ridge, Illinois, where she lived with her parents and brothers, Hugh Jr. and Tony.

In suburbia, women stayed home to look after the children, while men went to work. Both of Hillary's parents were strict Methodists who had lived through the Great Depression, when times were hard, and this is reflected in the way they raised their children. Hillary's father in particular was demanding and frugal. He wanted his children to learn to be personally and financially responsible.

Hillary attended Eugene Field Elementary School and Ralph Waldo Emerson Junior High School. Hillary loved school and was also a Brownie and later a Girl Scout. In fifth grade, she was elected cocaptain of the school's safety patrol—her first official elected position. Even at that young age, she had a talent for organizing people. She got groups of neighborhood kids together to put on carnivals and sporting events to raise money for charity. Hillary also played sports. She enjoyed playing softball and was a big fan of the Chicago Cubs baseball team.

Fear No One

Hillary's mother valued learning and encouraged her daughter to read books, taking her on weekly visits to the library. According to Hillary in her autobiography, *Living History*, although her mother "loved her home and her family, she felt limited by the narrow choices of her life." She wanted her daughter to be her own person and to succeed academically and professionally. She had seen intolerance first-hand during her childhood in California. There, Japanese American children were tormented by their white schoolmates because Japan had attacked America during World War II. She impressed on Hillary the need for tolerance and the importance of protecting others from discrimination.

She also insisted that Hillary learn to stick up for herself. As Hillary recounts in *Living History*, when she was four, she lived across the street from a girl named Suzy, who was used to playing rough with her brothers. She frequently bullied Hillary, and her mother worried that running away from her fears would set a bad pattern for Hillary later in life. Therefore, one day when Hillary sought refuge from Suzy by running into the house, her mother told her, "Go back out there, and if Suzy hits you, you have my permission to hit her back. You have to stand up for yourself. There's no room in this house for cowards." Hillary went back outside. When Suzy began to pick on her, Hillary stood up to her, returning triumphant and announcing, "I can play with the boys now. And Suzy will be my friend!"

Learning Responsibility

Hillary's father was a stern man who demanded much of his children. He felt that life was hard, and he insisted that they be strong enough to survive. He also hated wasting money. He ran his business on a cash basis, never relying on credit. He was strict about spending at home as well, punishing the children if he thought they were wasting anything and refusing to give them an allowance. He insisted that his children perform well in whatever they did, but he rarely praised them when they did so. He also emphasized the importance of understanding how to make money.

When she was old enough to do so, Hillary, like her brothers, helped out at Hugh's company. Her first real job came when she was thirteen. Three mornings a week, she supervised recreational activities at a small park for the Park Ridge Park District. From the age of thirteen on, she always worked over the summer and sometimes during the school year as well.

Hillary's mother was a Democrat, although according to Hillary, she kept quiet about this fact in the primarily conservative Park Ridge. Her father, in contrast, was a firmly conservative Republican. Hillary was deeply influenced both by the compassion and independence emphasized by her mother and by the conservative, survival-oriented attitude of her father.

High School

Hillary attended Maine Township High School East, a centralized school that drew its enrollment from a number of surrounding towns. When Hillary started high school, it had a student population of five thousand. Unlike her elementary school, whose population was entirely white and middle class, Maine East had students from a wide range of ethnic backgrounds

Pictured here is Maine Township High School, where Hillary attended school. During her high school years, Hillary was already showing a talent for leadership.

and economic classes. Hillary dressed like most girls of the day, in pleated skirts, blouses, and loafers. However, unlike many of the girls of the day, who were deeply concerned with attracting boys and future husbands, she wore no makeup and didn't worry much about her appearance. She was a good student who played field hockey and volleyball, as well as acted and sang in school performances. She played in a girls' summer softball league, wearing a uniform consisting of a pink shirt, black shorts, and white socks, because the team was sponsored by a local candy distributor selling Good & Plenty licorice candy. In *Living History*, she says of her high school, "It's a cliché now, but my high school in the 1960s resembled the movie *Grease* or the television show *Happy Days*." Then, as now, high school was an environment of distinct cliques. According to Hillary, there were "athletes and cheerleaders; student council types and brains; greasers and hoods." Because of confrontations between the different groups, the school authorities decided to set up the Cultural Values Committee. This was a student organization that included student representatives from all the different groups in the school. Its goal was to encourage mutual understanding and respect among the students. Dr. Clyde Watson, the principal, asked Hillary to serve on the committee. She credits her involvement in this program with allowing her to get to know kids she otherwise would have avoided. This approach—trying to bring together groups of people with disparate and opposing positions—is one she would continue to use throughout her professional life.

Competing with the Boys

Even at that young age, Hillary was a competitor, and in most of the organizations she was involved with she held a position at or near the top. She was president of the fan club for Fabian, a singer who was a teen idol of the time. She was also elected to the student council and successfully ran for junior class vice president. In her senior year, she became part of the first senior class at the newly built Maine Township High School South. There she ran for president of the student government, but lost. One of her opponents added insult to injury by telling her that she was stupid to think that a girl could be elected president.

President John F. Kennedy was elected in 1960, and he promoted a variety of social programs aimed at improving people's lives. He also supported initiatives designed to keep the United States technologically ahead of the Soviet Union. During World War II, the big threat to the United States had been the Nazis, who seemed intent on world domination. In the post–World War II years, Communism had replaced the Nazis as the major perceived threat to the United States. One of President Kennedy's most exciting initiatives was the space program. Hillary was fascinated by the idea of space travel, and when President Kennedy announced a goal to put men on the moon, she wrote a letter to NASA (the National Aeronautics and Space Administration) volunteering to join the astronaut-training program. When she

NATIONAL MERIT FINALISTS

received a response from NASA stating that the program didn't accept girls, she was furious.

Death of a President

Many people in the 1960s saw President Kennedy as a leader who would usher in an era of equality and new opportunities for all Americans. That dream ended abruptly, however. On November 22, 1963, a teacher came to inform Hillary's class that President John F. Kennedy had been shot in Dallas, Texas. Like the other students, she reacted with shock and disbelief. The principal dismissed the school early. At home she heard newscaster Walter Cronkite announce on TV that the president had died at 1:00 PM. The death of JFK left Hillary feeling sorry not only for his family but for the country as well. It inspired in her a desire to help make things better in some way, but she wasn't sure what to do.

How the Other Half Lives

The Rodhams attended the First United Methodist Church in Park Ridge. When Hillary was thirteen,

Hillary *(seated, front)* is pictured here as a teenager among other National Merit finalists. The National Merit award recognizes outstanding academic achievement.

the church appointed a new youth minister, Donald Jones, who had a lasting effect on Hillary's view of the world. In the 1960s, a new interest in social activism began to sweep the country, and Reverend Jones shared its values. He wanted to make the youth of Park Ridge more aware of the circumstances outside of their sheltered community and the need for social change. As part of his education in what he called "the University of Life," he took groups of teenagers, including Hillary, to Chicago's poor inner-city neighborhoods, where they met African American and Hispanic young people, including gang leaders. On one excursion he took them to see how migrant workers lived on nearby farms, and Hillary was among those who set up a babysitting project to care for the children while their parents labored in the fields. These experiences gave Hillary, for the first time, a sense of the hardships so many people had to deal with, and of how different her life was from theirs. From these contacts, she also learned about what was happening in the growing

John F. Kennedy served as the thirty-fifth president of the United States. For many Americans in the 1960s, President Kennedy's policies represented hope for a better way of life.

Pictured above is the First United Methodist Church where Hillary attended services while growing up. The church's youth program introduced her to the way that less fortunate people lived.

civil rights movement and its leader, Dr. Martin Luther King Jr. Through Reverend Jones she went to hear Dr. King give a speech at Chicago's Orchestra Hall, "Remaining Awake Through a Revolution," in which he emphasized the struggle for social change that was taking place and the need for all people to learn to live together or perish. Dr. King met with each of the students afterward, and Hillary was deeply impressed. Dr. King's speech opened her eyes to the civil rights struggle in America.

AuH₂O

The daughter of a staunch Republican in a firmly Republican town, Hillary also became an active member of the Young Republicans. A significant influence on her in this context was her ninth-grade history teacher, Paul Carlson. Carlson, a dedicated conservative and anti-Communist, encouraged her to read *The Conscience of a Conservative*, by Republican senator Barry Goldwater. During Goldwater's subsequent run for the presidency in 1964, Hillary became a "Goldwater Girl" and helped campaign for him locally. Goldwater supporters often wore buttons that said AuH_2O, a combination of the chemical symbols for gold (Au) and water (H_2O). Another high school teacher had a different influence on her views, however. Jerry Baker, a teacher on government, staged a mock debate during the 1964 campaign. Knowing that Hillary was a Republican and another student was a Democrat, he assigned them to argue the position of the opposing party. Faced with portraying the Democratic point of view, Hillary was forced to read up on then president Lyndon Johnson's positions on subjects such as civil rights, poverty, health care, and foreign policy. This exposed her to the other party's views for the first time.

Being a senior in high school meant that it was time for Hillary to plan her future. In 1965, she would graduate from high school. She needed to choose a college.

TWO NEW HORIZONS

Two women teaching government classes at Hillary's high school, Karin Fahlstrom and Janet Altman, encouraged her to go to a women's college. They felt that such colleges provided an environment in which women could focus on academics and have an opportunity to develop their leadership abilities. In co-ed colleges, social pressures encouraged girls to abandon such pursuits to men and take more traditional roles. Since Fahlstrom and Altman had attended Smith and Wellesley College, respectively, they naturally recommended that Hillary go to one of those schools. Both accepted her, but she

Wellesley College in Wellesley, Massachusetts, was founded in 1870. Wellesley's mission is to provide an excellent liberal arts education for women who will make a difference in the world.

was so charmed by photographs of the Wellesley campus, which is located about 15 miles (24 km) west of Boston, she chose that school.

When Hillary arrived in Massachusetts, it was one of the few times she had been away from home. Wellesley was a popular choice for the daughters of the affluent, and Hillary, with her middle-class background, found it intimidating at first. As she struggled with math and geology, she wondered if she could succeed there. In her autobiography, Hillary says, "A month after school started, I called

As class leader of Wellesley, Hillary, pictured here in 1969, gave the first commencement address by a student. In it she supported the need for students to protest negative government policies.

home collect and told my parents I didn't think I was smart enough to be there." Although her father encouraged her to come home, her mother told her not to be a quitter. After a few months, she got her feet under her and joined a number of clubs, in addition to pursuing her studies. Many of the courses she took reflected interests that would remain with her throughout her life, including child psychology and constitutional law. Still interested in politics, she was elected president of the college's Young Republicans. However, doubts about the validity of the Vietnam War, which was then raging, and questions about the party's position on civil rights soon led her to reevaluate her political allegiance, and she eventually resigned from that position.

Vietnam

In the mid-1960s, the country was deeply divided on the issue of the Vietnam War. As far back as 1954, the United States had been sending military "advisors" to South Vietnam. During the Cold War, many people, including many in the government, believed that if Communist North Vietnam succeeded in taking over democratic South Vietnam, the Communists would eventually take over the rest of Southeast Asia. Therefore, during the administrations

Young anti–Vietnam War protesters march in New York City in 1965. Many young men refused to fight in a war they considered unjust.

of four presidents, increasing numbers of troops were sent to Vietnam to fight alongside the South Vietnamese against the Communists. By the mid-1960s many opponents of the war were questioning (1) whether the United States should be in Vietnam, since war had never been officially declared by Congress, (2) whether the war could ever be won with the severe limitations imposed by its unofficial status, and (3) whether the threat of Communism spreading throughout Southeast Asia was as great as proponents of the war claimed. In contrast, those in favor of the war believed that not supporting it was unpatriotic, and that the threat from the Communists was real. The passion of both sides resulted in increasingly violent confrontations and protests.

By 1967, these protests had spread to college campuses around the United States. In her junior year, 1967–1968, Hillary switched from being a "young Republican" to canvassing for Democratic senator Eugene McCarthy from Minnesota, who was running for the Democratic presidential nomination. McCarthy was a vocal opponent of the war.

Death of Another Dream

On April 4, 1968, Dr. Martin Luther King Jr. was assassinated in Memphis, Tennessee, by James Earl Ray. Hillary was distraught when she heard the news. She joined other women from Wellesley participating in a memorial march in Boston, wearing black armbands. Dr. King's death galvanized her feelings about civil rights. The assassination of Senator Robert Kennedy on June 5, 1968, further increased her angst about what was happening in America. Feeling that the university wasn't doing enough, she ran for president of the student government. She campaigned for more student control over university policies. Much to her amazement, she won.

In her sophomore year, 1966–1967, only a handful of African American women were part of the student body of Wellesley. Hillary joined the students advocating greater enrollment of black women. A number of black students had started Ethos, the first African American organization at Wellesley. In the wake of Dr. King's assassination, the members of Ethos demanded that the Wellesley administration recruit more black students and faculty, threatening a hunger strike if they refused. When dialogue between the students and the administration threatened to erupt into confrontation, Ethos requested Hillary, as student government president, to get the administration to address their grievances. Once again, Hillary found herself acting as mediator between opposing factions. The Wellesley administration did ultimately make an attempt to recruit more minorities, and her activities gave her an increased awareness of the plight of African Americans, not only on the political level but also individually. One of her volunteer extracurricular activities was reading to poor black children in Roxbury, the ghetto area of Boston.

First Dip in the Political Pool

In 1968, Hillary was encouraged to apply for the Wellesley in Washington program by the program's director, Professor Alan Shechter, who taught political science at Wellesley. According to Hillary, he knew she was moving toward more liberal views and thought the experience would help her clarify her own political position. She was chosen from three hundred applicants to be one of thirty students to go to Washington, D.C., as interns. Over the summer, she worked for a congressional group led by Congressmen Melvin Laird of Wisconsin, Charles Goodell of New York, and then minority leader Gerald Ford. The job gave her the chance to research and write about congressional issues. After her internship, she went to the Republican National Convention in Miami, where a Republican candidate for president would be chosen. She worked for the nomination of Nelson Rockefeller, a moderate Republican who was in favor of ending the Vietnam War and addressing social problems. Rockefeller lost the nomination to the more conservative Richard M. Nixon. However, working at the convention was Hillary's first real experience with national politics.

The 1968 Democratic National Convention was even more of an eye-opener for Hillary. It was held in Chicago, and Hillary was at home in Park Ridge at the time. While watching it on TV, she saw the historic violent confrontation between a large mass of protesters and the Chicago police. With her friend Betsy Johnson, she immediately went down-town to Grant Park, where the melee was taking place. The police brutality she saw shocked her profoundly and emphasized how sheltered she'd been in Park Ridge.

After graduating in 1969, Hillary spent the summer working her way across Alaska in a variety of jobs

A Chicago police officer confronts a protester outside Democratic Party headquarters in Chicago during the 1968 Democratic Convention. The brutal way police treated protesters shocked many people.

The First Student Speaker

Hillary had the distinction of being the first student to give a commencement address at Wellesley College. She spoke about a number of issues of concern to young people coming of age in a deeply divided country, saying, "We're not in the positions yet of leadership and power, but we do have that indispensable task of criticizing and constructive protest." She went on to defend the need to demand change when addressing inequities and the need to ask questions about U.S. institutions and the government. However, she also emphasized the importance of integrity, trust, and respect among people. These are attitudes that she has carried with her into her adult political life—trying to implement change where she perceives it is needed, but choosing to work with her opponents to achieve her goals. Hillary's commencement address was featured in a *Life* magazine article covering the graduating students of 1969.

that included sliming salmon on the pier in Valdez. She was then ready for the next step in her academic and political education.

27 out of 235

In 1969, Hillary entered Yale Law School in New Haven, Connecticut. In a class of 235, she was one of twenty-seven female students. She received a partial scholarship from Wellesley and paid for the rest of her education with loans. She was a dedicated, serious student who served on the editorial board of the Yale *Review of Law and Social Action*. She also remained involved in social protest. By the late 1960s, protests were becoming even more confrontational. Activist groups such as the Weathermen and the Black Panthers had begun to use violence as a means to force social change they felt could not be achieved by protests alone. When a group of Black Panthers was put on trial in New Haven, Hillary was involved in organizing groups of students to monitor the trial to make sure there were no civil rights violations.

In April 1970, President Nixon announced he was expanding the Vietnam War by sending troops into Cambodia. In May, four students at Kent State University were shot by National Guard troops while protesting the war. Hillary subsequently moderated a mass meeting where Yale law students voted 239–12 to join students at three hundred colleges around the country in a national strike to protest the United States' involvement in the war.

Civil Rights

On May 7, 1970, Hillary spoke at the convention of the League of Women Voters in Washington, D.C.

Wearing a black armband in memory of the dead Kent State students, she spoke about how the expansion of the Vietnam War had motivated the previously uninvolved Yale law students to join other students around the country in protest.

It was at the league convention that Hillary met Marian Wright Edelman. An alumna of Yale Law School, Edelman was the first black woman in Mississippi to be admitted to practice law. She had run the NAACP Legal Defense and Education Fund office in Jackson, Mississippi, throughout the mid-1960s and was heavily involved in the civil rights movement. From Edelman's husband, Peter, an ex-aide to Senator Robert Kennedy, Hillary learned that Edelman planned to form an organization to fight poverty. When Edelman came to speak at Yale a few months later, Hillary asked her for a summer job. Edelman agreed but had no funds to pay her. Hillary applied for a grant from the Law Student Civil Rights Research Council and received enough funding to allow her to spend the summer of 1970 working in Washington, D.C., at Marian Edelman's Washington Research Project. There she was engaged in researching the plight of the children of migrant workers, a project harkening back to her youthful experience with itinerant farm workers.

Returning to Yale with a newfound interest in children's rights, she decided to spend an extra year there studying child development at the Yale Child Study Center. She acted as research assistant to the center's director, Dr. Al Solnit, and Professor Joe Stein on their book *Beyond the Best Interests of the Child.* She also consulted at Yale-New Haven Hospital on legal procedures for dealing with suspected child abuse. As a result of her combined interest in child welfare and the law, she wrote her first scholarly article, "Children Under the Law," which was published in the *Harvard Educational Review* in 1974. Hillary was about to encounter more than academics at Yale, however.

Finding True Love

One night in 1970, Hillary was studying at the Yale law library when she noticed a good-looking young man standing in the hall. He was talking to another student, but he kept looking over at her. Finally she got up, walked over to him, and said, "If you're going to keep looking at me, and I'm going to keep looking back, we might as well be introduced. I'm Hillary Rodham." According to Bill Clinton, he was so flustered that he couldn't remember his name. The next time they saw each other was the last day

of classes. When Hillary told him she was on her way to register for the next semester's courses, Bill told her he was heading over to the registrar's office, too. This worked fine as a ploy, until they reached the front of the line and the registrar said, "What are you doing here, Bill? You've already registered." He was forced to admit that he simply wanted to spend time with Hillary. Not long after, Bill called Hillary, only to find out that she had come down with a terrible cold. He showed up in her room with chicken soup and orange juice, and the couple soon became inseparable.

Moving Together and Apart

Bill, already preparing for a career in politics, had been planning to spend the summer working in the South for Democratic senator George McGovern's presidential campaign. However, when he found out that Hillary was going to work as a clerk at the law firm of Treuhaft, Walker and Burnstein in Oakland, California, he announced that he was going to go to California, too. At the end of the summer, when

Bill and Hillary are pictured here at Yale University in the 1970s. Hillary met Bill during her first year, upon his return from studying at Oxford University in England.

they returned from California, they moved together into a $75-a-month apartment in New Haven. Like many students, they furnished the place with furniture they bought at thrift shops.

As with most couples, there was also the ordeal of meeting each other's parents. Bill charmed Hillary's mother. Her father took longer to warm up to the Democrat from Arkansas, although eventually they found a mutual interest in cards and football. Hillary made even less of a good impression on Bill's mother, Virginia (his father had died three months before he was born). Virginia was a southern woman with firm beliefs about what a lady should look like—including makeup, hairstyle, and nice clothes. According to Bill Clinton in his autobiography, *My Life*, "With no makeup, a work shirt and jeans, and bare feet coated with tar from walking on the beach at Milford, she [Hillary] might as well have been a space alien. The fact that I was obviously serious about her gave Mother heartburn." Over time, Hillary and Virginia's relationship became more cordial.

When they graduated in 1973, Bill took Hillary on a trip to the United Kingdom. He had studied at Oxford University, and now he took her to see England and Wales. It was Hillary's first trip to Europe.

In the Lake District of England, Bill asked Hillary to marry him. Although she was in love with him, she was uncertain, responding, "No, not now." Bill would ask her to marry him repeatedly, until finally he declared that he wasn't going to ask anymore. He told her, "If you ever decide you want to marry me, then you have to tell me." He was heading home to Arkansas, while Hillary would stay on the East Coast for her first real job. First, however, she took a trip with Bill to Arkansas, where, at his insistence, she took the bar exam that would allow her to practice law in Arkansas . . . just in case.

THREE

FACING THE REAL WORLD

While Bill returned to Arkansas to teach at the University of Arkansas School of Law, Hillary took her first full-time job—as a lawyer for Marian Wright Edelman's Children's Defense Fund (CDF) in Cambridge, Massachusetts. The fund sought to improve the conditions of minority children and those who were handicapped or living in poverty. In this position, Hillary investigated and fought to improve conditions under which juvenile offenders were imprisoned in South Carolina. She also discovered that in Massachusetts many children with physical disabilities were not receiving an education.

The CDF and other groups lobbied Congress, which eventually passed the Education for All Handicapped Children Act, requiring public schools to educate disabled children.

Impeaching a President

On June 17, 1972, five men broke into the Democratic National Party headquarters at the plush Watergate complex in Washington, D.C., intending to plant electronic bugs and possibly photograph documents. Investigations subsequently revealed that President

Richard M. Nixon, thirty-seventh president of the United States, says good-bye to his staff on August 9, 1974 after resigning because of the Watergate scandal.

Richard M. Nixon had knowledge of the plan and had tried to cover it up. As a result, in early 1974, John Doar, chief counsel to the House Judiciary Committee, was charged with drawing up articles of impeachment against the president. Hillary was asked to be one of the forty-four lawyers who would do research for the impeachment proceedings. She left Cambridge and went to Washington. The lawyers worked in the Old Congressional Hotel. According to Hillary, "most of us were young, eager law school graduates who were willing to work

Hillary is pictured here working with the House committee on President Nixon's impeachment. This work made her familiar with the rigorous requirements that should be met to impeach a president.

twenty-hour days in makeshift offices, reviewing documents, researching and transcribing tapes." On August 9, 1974, President Nixon resigned, making impeachment unnecessary, and Hillary's job ended. What she did next surprised her friends.

A Woman Lawyer in Arkansas

Hillary went to Arkansas to be with Bill. Some of her friends thought she was crazy to leave the East Coast, where she could pursue a high-powered career. Nonetheless, she followed her heart. She was hired by the University of Arkansas School of Law to teach criminal law and trial advocacy as well as run the legal aid clinic and prison projects. At the time, there was only one other woman on the faculty. Working as a woman lawyer in Arkansas was something of a culture shock for Hillary. Once when she was defending a legal aid client—a man accused of a sex crime—the judge asked her to leave the room because he "couldn't talk about such things in front of a lady." Hillary had to convince him that, as the defendant's lawyer, she had to stay.

One of the problems she faced running the legal clinic was that an old law, on the books since the 1800s, allowed a defendant to have free legal representation only when his assets were worth less than $10. That old law was used by some judges to block law students from defending poor clients. Hillary enlisted Vince Foster of the Rose Law Firm, one of the oldest in the area, to help her get the law repealed.

Making a Home

When school ended, Hillary decided to take a trip back home. As Bill was driving her to the airport, they passed a small brick house that was for sale, and Hillary remarked how sweet she thought it was. She visited friends in Boston, New York, Washington, and Park Ridge. The trip left her convinced that what she really wanted to do was return to Bill in Arkansas. This was a good thing because when Bill picked her up at the airport, he said, "Remember that little house you liked so much? I bought it. You have to marry me now because I can't live there alone." On October 11, 1975, they were married in the living room of that house. Hillary kept her own last name when she married Bill because she used her name professionally and wanted to be judged on her own merits. It was a decision that immediately caused consternation among Bill's family and would later cause greater controversy when Bill took to the campaign trail to become governor of Arkansas.

New Jobs

While Hillary was working in Washington, Bill Clinton had run and lost his first political race—to be a congressman from Arkansas. In 1976, he ran for attorney general of Arkansas, and this time he had no problem winning. Once he won the primary, he had no Republican opponent. The fact that his election was assured left Hillary free to campaign for Jimmy Carter's election as president, and at the request of Carter's staff she became the field coordinator for Indiana. In that job she was responsible for setting up individual campaigns in the various counties around the state. Jimmy Carter won the election, although he didn't carry the state of Indiana. However, his election meant that Hillary was now free to look for another job. It was clear that she was going to be the one responsible for providing support for her family. Although it was becoming obvious that Bill had qualities that made it likely he would succeed in politics, his job as attorney general paid only $26,500 a year. Another consideration in Hillary's job search was the need to avoid any conflicts of interest that would make it look as if she were receiving unfair benefits by being married to the state attorney general. For that reason, she decided to steer clear of state-related jobs, such as working as a prosecutor. Instead, she took a job as a lawyer at the Rose Law Firm. The firm got a ruling from the Arkansas Bar Association stating that it could hire the wife of the attorney general, and it spelled out exactly what steps she had to take to avoid any conflicts of interest. She was the first woman lawyer hired by the firm.

One of the areas in which Hillary became involved was, again, children's welfare. She fought for the right of foster parents to adopt children placed in their care, something denied by state law. She was one of the group of Arkansans who founded the Arkansas Advocates for Children and Families, an organization that fights for the welfare of children in courts.

Bill followed his run for attorney general with a successful campaign for governor in 1978. In 1979, Bill called on Hillary to head a forty-four-member committee called the Rural Health Advisory Committee. Their job was to develop a way to provide health care to people in isolated areas around the state. The committee succeeded in developing a network of health clinics in rural areas. That year Hillary was also appointed by President Carter to the board of the U.S. Legal Services Corporation. This was a project formed by Congress under President Nixon to provide legal aid to the poor.

Feathering a Nest

During this time, Hillary had more personal matters on her mind, however. She and Bill had decided to start a family. Once that decision was made, she immediately began worrying about how they were going to support children. Since Bill's salary was dependent on his staying in office, and there was no guarantee of that, Hillary decided to try to develop a nest egg they could depend on if necessary. The husband of one of her friends was lawyer Jim Blair, and he had expertise in the commodities market. The commodities market is much like the stock market, except that, instead of buying and selling shares in companies, traders buy and sell contracts that give them ownership of commodities such as coffee or cattle. They buy the contract for an amount of the commodity at a given price and then sell the contract for a profit to someone else who thinks the commodity will be worth more by the time it is delivered. With Jim Blair's assistance, Hillary traded cattle commodities so successfully that she turned her initial $1,000 into $100,000. Then she got out of the market. At the same time, she and Bill invested some money in a real estate development in Arkansas with local businessman Jim McDougal. They quickly lost money on the property, called Whitewater Estates. This deal would come back to haunt them years later.

Starting a Family

Bill and Hillary had been trying to have a child for some time when Hillary finally became pregnant in 1979. Toward the end of her pregnancy, her doctor advised her against traveling, so in February 1980, Bill went alone to Washington, D.C., for the annual White House governors' dinner. He arrived home just as Hillary went into labor. One of the stories that both Clintons tell is that they had been attending birthing classes together, like any young couple. As a result, they had a list of things they were supposed to take to the hospital. One thing on the list was a bag of ice for Hillary to suck on

Governor Bill Clinton and First Lady of Arkansas Hillary Rodham attend a 1979 dinner at the White House honoring the nation's governors.

while she was in labor. When she went into labor, however, both the governor and the protective detail of state troopers were so flustered, that, as she got into the car, Hillary saw a trooper putting a trash bag containing nine pounds of ice into the trunk.

Hillary gave birth to Chelsea Victoria Clinton on February 27, 1980. Chelsea was so named because during a Christmas visit to England in 1978, Hillary and Bill had been strolling around Chelsea in London while listening to Judy Collins's version of the song "Chelsea Morning," written by Joni Mitchell.

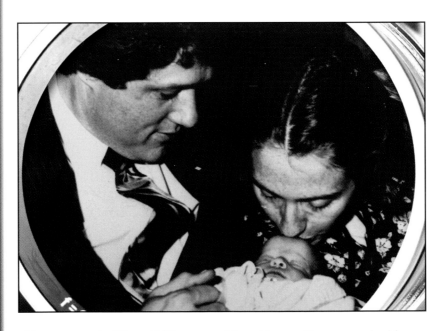

Happy parents Bill and Hillary are pictured here with one-week-old Chelsea on March 5, 1980. Having a child of her own reinforced Hillary's feeling about how vulnerable children are.

Bill said that if they ever had a daughter, they should name her Chelsea.

Hillary reacted to Chelsea's birth like most first-time mothers—with great love, but complete inexperience. In *The Unique Voice of Hillary Rodham Clinton*, by Claire G. Osborne, Hillary is quoted as saying, "I remember when I was breast-feeding Chelsea when I was still in the hospital. I had her head tilted at a funny angle and the milk started to come out of her nose. I thought I was killing my baby. I was just in a panic, you know, I was just really upset. And this wonderful old nurse came in and said, 'Well, if you hold her up a little higher, that won't happen.'"

Hillary would have liked to have more children, but that was not to happen.

Changes of Identity

The governor is elected for a two-year term in Arkansas. Bill had another election coming up in 1980, and this time he lost. Some of Bill's supporters started to pressure Hillary to change her last name to Clinton. Some people in Arkansas were offended by her refusing to change her name; others were bothered by receiving invitations from the governor and "Hillary Rodham." Chelsea's birth announcement

It Takes a Village

Hillary had always been interested in the welfare of children, but having a child of one's own gives one a new perspective on life. Raising Chelsea taught Hillary that many people throughout a community contribute to the child-rearing process. In 1996, she wrote a book on raising a child that she titled *It Takes a Village*, after the African proverb "It takes a village to raise a child." As she says in the book, children "depend on adults they know and thousands more who make decisions every day that affect their well-being." Hillary acknowledges that parents have the primary responsibility for raising their children. However, she emphasizes that people and institutions in the community and government play a vital role in ensuring that children grow up healthy and secure. Although this would seem like a laudable position, not everyone approved of her views. Many conservatives saw the book as supporting government intervention in the family, and some accused her of trying to promote socialism (considered by critics to be a milder form of Communism) in raising children.

When she went on tour to promote the book, she was met with an extremely positive reaction from parents who were concerned about the difficulties of raising children without adequate support in a culture that subjects children to a vast array of negative pressures. Hillary donated 100 percent of the money she received from the book to children's charities—a sum that ultimately reached $1 million.

Above, Hillary signs copies of *It Takes a Village*. Parents around the country responded positively to the idea that it takes efforts from the entire community to successfully raise a child.

from Bill Clinton and Hillary Rodham caused even more of a stir. Although Bill never asked her to change her name, she decided that doing so would contribute to his chances of retaking the governorship in the next election, so she became Hillary Rodham Clinton. It would not be the last time that those in political circles would pressure her to conform. Bill, Hillary, and Chelsea drove around the entire state of Arkansas during the campaign. They met with groups of Arkansans face to face in towns across the state to convince them to vote for Bill. Bill won the next gubernatorial race, and the Clintons retained the governor's mansion through the rest of the 1980s. However, the start of the new decade brought them broader horizons.

FOUR

THE WHITE HOUSE YEARS

In her autobiography, *Living History*, Hillary says about Bill's run for the presidency in 1992, "If the first forty-four years of my life were an education, the thirteen-month presidential campaign was a revelation." Being in the intense scrutiny of national media was a new and stressful experience. When the campaign began, Hillary did something previously unheard of. In prior presidential campaigns, the candidate's campaign staff had also taken charge of his wife's schedule and controlled what she said. Not so with Hillary. She assembled her own staff to manage her part in the campaign.

Hillary and Bill along with Al and Tipper Gore greet supporters in Corsicana, Texas, during the candidates' cross-country bus trip while campaigning for election in 1992.

In order to avoid the appearance of being tied to any special interest and to devote herself full-time to the campaign, Hillary had to resign from the boards of the charitable and corporate organizations on which she served, including the Children's Defense Fund. She also took a leave of absence from the Rose Law Firm. It was the first time in her adult life that her sole role was to be a wife. The campaign required Hillary, Bill, prospective vice president Al Gore, and his wife, Tipper, to travel the country in a customized bus, making campaign stops all along the way. From the beginning, the public was uncertain how to take Hillary. Her supporters admired her for being a strong woman who wasn't afraid to have her own life and opinions. Her detractors thought she was a strident feminist who had aspirations to be copresident. Bill fueled this belief by implying that if he were elected, the presidency would in reality be a partnership, with Hillary having a role in making policy. Those who wanted to see women taking a more active role in public life were thrilled. Those who believed women should stay in more traditional roles were appalled. Nonetheless, on November 3, 1992, Bill Clinton was elected the forty-second president. Hillary was now First Lady of not just one state but of the entire United States. And a unique First Lady she would turn out to be.

The Job with No Description

Once she arrived in Washington, Hillary was faced with a quandary experienced by all First Ladies— what was her role? Unlike the president and vice president, who have specific tasks assigned to them, there is no job description for being a First Lady. Yet she cannot remain totally in the background. Simply by virtue of being the First Lady she is both a symbol of and ambassador for the president. Hillary was a

first in the White House—a First Lady who was a professional in her own right. She was not, however, as some have suggested, the only First Lady to take an avid interest in the policies of her husband's administration. As far back as the administration of John Adams, the second president, Abigail Adams advised her husband on political issues, a fact that was noted in her day. Indeed, a woman Hillary is known to admire, Eleanor Roosevelt, was famous for her advocacy for social programs during Franklin Roosevelt's four terms in office. The significant part played by previous First Ladies has been largely left out of the history books. With the exception of Eleanor Roosevelt, most First Ladies pursued their agendas quietly behind the scenes or on the fringes of the presidency. Not so with Hillary. To begin with, previous First Ladies had all had offices in the East Wing of the White House, with minimal staff, whereas the president's office and staff are located in the West Wing. Hillary was the first First Lady to have an office in the West Wing, where the real work of the government takes place. Second, no

Bill and Hillary host a formal affair at the White House for visiting dignitaries. Hosting foreign visitors is an important part of a First Lady's duties.

In the West Wing, Hillary talks with reporters about health care reform. Ultimately the health care reform package proved too massive and controversial for Congress to accept.

First Lady prior to Hillary had been given responsibility for a major policy area. Bill Clinton gave Hillary the responsibility of putting together a major health care reform package, designed to cover a wide range of health care issues. These included such issues as the lack of affordable health insurance, the rising costs of medical treatment, and the loss of coverage for people who are switching jobs. Many of Hillary's detractors objected to her nontraditional role. Some accused her of not being interested in performing the traditional duties of a First Lady, such as overseeing the state dinners and entertaining visiting dignitaries. Hillary, however, was a woman of her generation. Like so many working mothers, hers wasn't a choice between being a professional or being a wife and mother. She was both. As Hillary puts it in *Living History*, "I cared about the food I served our guests, and I also wanted to improve the delivery of health care to all Americans." One of the innovations she would make in White House celebrations was the inclusion of menorahs in the display of Christmas trees featured in the White House every year.

Although Hillary ultimately lost the battle to get Congress to accept health care reform, this effort incorporated a process she would later use more successfully in her campaign for the Senate. She traveled all around the country talking to people and listening to their difficulties with the health care system.

Meanwhile, Hillary would have liked Chelsea to attend public school, but that proved impractical. The need for the Secret Service to protect her, and the fact that her parents didn't want her to be constantly pestered by the media, meant that she needed to be in an environment where the access of outsiders could be controlled. Therefore, they enrolled Chelsea in the Sidwell Friends Quaker School. During school holidays, however, Chelsea often traveled with her

Hillary speaks at the White House, June 27, 1992. Hillary was involved in policy making in a way that no First Lady before her was.

Raising a Teenager in the White House

Hillary and Bill with Chelsea at her high school graduation in 1997

Chelsea was eleven years old when her father became president. Since Bill had been important in politics as the governor of Arkansas, even before he ran for president, one of the issues that Hillary had to grapple with was how to give Chelsea a normal childhood. While Bill was governor, she and Bill shielded Chelsea from the press as much as possible. During the presidential campaign, they had limited the press's contact with Chelsea to times when she appeared in public with her parents. Now that Bill was president, scrutiny of his family was bound to increase. Unsure how best to approach raising a child in the White House, Hillary turned to an expert on the subject. She visited Jacqueline Kennedy Onassis, the widow of President John F. Kennedy, in New York. Jackie advised Hillary to surround Chelsea with supportive family and friends without spoiling her, to keep the press away from her, and generally to keep her from feeling privileged or entitled.

mother on trips overseas relating to women's and children's welfare. These trips gave her an invaluable education in what people's lives are like in other parts of the world. The Secret Service's code name for Chelsea was "Energy."

Scandals and Vindication

While Bill and Hillary were campaigning, Jim McDougal, their old partner in Whitewater Estates, was indicted for fraud and other crimes. Not long after Bill Clinton became president, conservative Republicans started searching for some way to discredit him and disrupt the implementation of social programs such as health care reform and other expanded public benefits. Some of these people were against the expansion of such programs because they believed that government should play only a limited role in citizens' lives, and they saw these projects as a form of socialism. Others were simply political oppor- tunists who feared that if the president succeeded in getting such reforms passed, the Republican Party would lose the presidency and congressional seats to the Democrats for a long time to come. Whatever their rationale, they fixed on Jim McDougal and Whitewater as the means to derail the president's agenda. They attempted to prove that Bill and Hillary's investment in Whitewater meant they were involved in McDougal's illegal schemes. The result was an eight-year investigation that cost taxpayers

$70 million and found in the end that neither Bill nor Hillary had committed any wrongdoing.

Life Under the Microscope

The Whitewater investigations had a profound effect on Hillary in several ways. First, she had to live through eight years of accusations about the role she played not only in Whitewater, but in her investments and her activities with the Rose Law Firm. As might be expected, this was extremely stressful. Second, in the course of asking the president questions for a grand jury hearing, the special prosecutor appointed to lead the investigation, Kenneth Starr, accused him of having an affair with a woman named Monica Lewinsky, who worked as an intern in the White House. Although Bill denied it, he was later forced to admit that the accusation was true. Because he was under oath at the time he made his denial, Kenneth Starr was able to use his lie as an excuse to start impeachment proceedings. Impeachment is the indictment of a president by the House of Representatives, for trial by the Senate. Ultimately, the Senate's vote did not even come close to the two-thirds needed to remove the president from office.

The revelation that her husband had cheated on her upset Hillary terribly, but she decided not to let it destroy her marriage. Her decision to stand by Bill caused yet another uproar. Some people felt outraged that she didn't leave Bill; others lauded her for staying. Ironically, however, it helped her political image by making her appear a more sympathetic figure. The experience also toughened Hillary up. After eight years of hounding and the relentless examination of every aspect of her personal and professional life, Hillary was certainly well prepared to withstand anything future campaigns would throw at her.

THE WELFARE OF MILLIONS

Hillary spent a significant amount of her time in the White House working for the improvement of conditions under which women and children live. Being the First Lady gave her an unequaled opportunity to fight for women's and children's rights and welfare, not only in the United States but worldwide.

Health Care Revisited

After the defeat of the massive health care bill, Hillary continued to work on smaller pieces of the health care puzzle. She worked quietly with Senator Edward Kennedy of Massachusetts on the Children's Health Insurance

Program (CHIP). This program guarantees health insurance to children whose families make too much money to qualify for Medicaid (the health insurance program that provides health care coverage for the poor) but too little to afford to pay for health insurance themselves. By 2003, more than five million children were covered by this program. She also championed a bill to increase the number of children who receive childhood vaccinations. Hillary worked for bills that guaranteed that women would be allowed to stay in the hospital for more than twenty-four hours after giving birth and that covered mammograms to protect women against breast cancer. In 1995, she implemented the Medicare Mammography Awareness Campaign to encourage older women to get mammograms, which can detect breast cancer.

International Affairs

In her role as First Lady, Hillary had the opportunity to travel to many countries. For example, in January of 1994, Hillary traveled with Bill to Russia, where they met with then president Boris Yeltsin and his wife, Naini. Later that year, she headed the American delegation to the 1994 Olympic Games in Lillehammer, Norway. During the visit she met with Gro Brundtland,

Bill and Hillary meet with Russian president Boris Yeltsin at an official dinner in Moscow in 1994. As First Lady, Hillary had the opportunity to meet many world leaders.

prime minister of Norway, who later became head of the World Health Organization.

In 1994, Hillary accompanied Vice President Al Gore and his wife, Tipper, on a trip to South Africa to be present at the historic swearing in of Nelson Mandela as president of a newly desegregated South Africa. During Bill's first term, Hillary had the opportunity to meet Yitzhak Rabin, then prime minister of Israel, and his wife, Leah. Late in 1994, she visited Egypt, Israel, and Jordan while the president was trying to broker a peace treaty between Arabs and Israelis in the Middle East. The trip gave her a first-hand look at the difficulties faced by leaders of nations where part of the populace is Western-educated and wants to modernize the country, while other people are equally determined to hold on to their traditional ways of life.

Hillary would later travel to countries such as Bosnia-Herzegovina, the Czech Republic, and Romania to show America's support for those attempting to establish sound democratic societies in the aftermath of war, turmoil, and upheaval. In Northern Ireland, while Bill met with Catholic and Protestant leaders, she met with a group of Catholic and Protestant women attempting to work together to end the violence there.

Women's Welfare, Human Rights

Some of Hillary's most important international visits during Bill's presidency focused on the welfare of women around the world. For example, in March 1995, Hillary embarked on a twelve-day visit to

Hillary, accompanied by Chelsea, receives a garland from a girl during a 1995 tour of a children's home in New Delhi, India. Hillary was active in children's welfare issues worldwide.

Southeast Asia, where she visited five countries: Pakistan, India, Sri Lanka, Bangladesh, and Nepal. The purpose of the trip was to demonstrate support for leaders in the area who supported democracy and to promote efforts to improve human rights. Hillary was particularly interested in the rights of women, and she took the opportunity to emphasize the relationship between women's rights and a country's prosperity. In her autobiography, *Living History*, Hillary says that in Southeast Asia she found that "poor women and girls are oppressed and discriminated against, denied education and medical care and victimized by culturally sanctioned violence."

Her itinerary took her not just to presidential palaces but to the villages in the countries she visited. She found that in supposedly democratic countries, such as Pakistan, even upper-class women could often only do things their husbands allowed them to do. At the same time, schools for girls and colleges for women were allowing women, for the first time, to gain the knowledge to start their own businesses.

In India she visited one of Mother Teresa's orphanages, where she found that many poor families abandoned girl babies at the orphanage because

Hillary meets with Mother Teresa in Washington in honor of the opening of the Mother Teresa Home for Infant Children in 1995.

their resources were limited and boys were more valued than girls. (In some cultures like India, where a woman joins her husband's family after marriage, raising girls is often seen as simply using up resources to raise a child for someone else's family.) In India she

CAREER PROFILES

Hillary and Eleanor

It's a well-known fact that Hillary admires Eleanor Roosevelt. One of her habits when trying to hash out a problem is to hold an imaginary conversation with Eleanor. Like Hillary, Eleanor Roosevelt was a tireless campaigner for social issues. She was a champion of causes such as civil rights, refugees, child labor laws, and the welfare of women both in the United States and

Eleanor Roosevelt (1884–1962) was a voice for the underprivileged.

internationally. Like Hillary, she traveled the country and the world, rallying people to her causes, and pressed the president to support them. In her day, she too faced criticism from the press, and sometimes from her husband Franklin's advisors, for being too outspoken. Like Hillary, she was a writer and wrote a number of books about her experiences, including *This Is My Story* (1937), *This I Remember* (1950), *On My Own* (1958), and *Tomorrow Is Now* (published posthumously, 1963). She also penned a newspaper column called "My Day" from the time her husband held the presidency until 1962. During her time in the White House, Hillary, too, wrote a syndicated newspaper column, called "Talking It Over," and she had a bust of Eleanor added to the Roosevelt Room in the White House.

met with Ela Bhatt, head of the Self-Employed Women's Association (SEWA). SEWA gives Indian women small loans, which they use to start their own businesses, such as setting up stalls in the market to sell vegetables or other goods. Such micro-lending programs have long been a major area of interest to Hillary. She visited Bangladesh with the Grameen Bank, which has provided millions of dollars of micro-credit loans to poor women. In 2006, Muhammad Yunus, who founded the Grameen Bank, received the Nobel Peace Prize for his work in providing funding to the poor worldwide.

Speaking for Women in China

In 1995, Hillary attended the UN Fourth World Conference on Women in Beijing, China, as honorary chairperson of the U.S. delegation. At the convention, she emphasized that women's rights are basic human rights, not some separate sub-category of human rights. She emphasized that violence against women in all its forms is a violation of human rights. And she insisted that women have the right to education, health care, legal services, and political inclusion.

Hillary had the opportunity to visit many other places during her time as First Lady. Her exposure

Hillary spoke on "Women and Health" at the UN Fourth World Conference on Women in Beijing, China, urging the Chinese to take action to ensure women access to health care.

to and involvement in political issues around the world has given her valuable insight into the issues that face people worldwide, as well as a useful network of political contacts.

S I X
A Political Life of Her Own

Toward the end of Bill Clinton's second term as president, Daniel Moynihan, a longtime senator from New York, announced his retirement. High-ranking members of the Democratic Party soon began feeling out Hillary to see if she would be interested in running for the Senate. If she did so and won, she would be the first First Lady to hold a major political position in her own right. There were two considerations Hillary had to grapple with: First, if she ran, she would be campaigning during the end of Bill's last term in office. Somehow she would have to address the duties of being both the First Lady and a candidate.

Second, New York is a state of 54,000 square miles, with a population of 19 million people. She would have to cover a lot of ground and convince a large and diverse population that she could represent their interests.

Adding to the potential difficulties was the fact that no woman had ever won a statewide office in New York. There were easier—and more lucrative— jobs she could have taken. She had potential opportunities to become the head of a charitable foundation, a corporate CEO, president of a college, or even a talk show host. In addition, campaigning meant a grueling schedule and being constantly on the road. Nonetheless, she decided to take the plunge.

On the Campaign Trail Again

Hillary and Bill bought a house in New York state, where they planned to live after Bill completed his term as president. However, since Hillary was not a native of New York, she had her work cut out for her to convince the citizens of the state that she could legitimately represent them. She traveled the length and breadth of the state listening to people's concerns. For instance, a critical issue for people in upstate New York was help in revitalizing their stalled economy. For a year, Hillary drove back and

As a senatorial candidate, Hillary is greeted on Election Day, November 7, 2000, by supporters wearing Hillary masks in Chappaqua, New York, where she now lives.

forth throughout New York state, determined to have face-to-face meetings with her potential constituents in every one of the state's sixty-two counties.

She officially declared her candidacy in February 2000 at the University of New York, in Purchase, New York. Hillary couldn't adequately campaign for the Senate and fulfill her duties as First Lady, however. Therefore, Chelsea, who had taken extra credits at Stamford, came home from college and spent several months dividing her time between assisting her father in the White House and her mother in her campaign for the Senate. Hillary began the race running against Mayor Rudolph Giuliani of New York City. When the mayor was forced to drop out of the race for medical reasons, Hillary found herself having to adapt to running against a new opponent, New York congressman Rick Lazio, a conservative Republican. While Lazio ran a negative campaign against Hillary, she stayed focused on the issues. While he was talking about Hillary, she was talking about things that mattered to the people who would vote, including the local economy, health care, education, Social Security, and other meaty issues. This strategy worked. Hillary won the election, getting 55 percent of the vote to Lazio's 43 percent. But her work was just beginning.

Senator Clinton

On January 3, 2001, Hillary was sworn in as the junior senator from New York. She was not only the first First Lady to hold an elected political office, but also the first woman elected to a statewide office in New York. Hillary serves on the Senate Armed Services Committee; the Health, Labor and Pensions Committee; the Environment and Public Works Committee; and the Senate Special Committee on Aging.

The November 8, 2000, edition of the *Chicago Sun-Times*, Hillary's hometown newspaper, trumpets her victory in the New York Senate race.

Nov. 8, 2000

2000
Chicago Sun-Times

MIDWEST'S BEST-READ NEWSPAPER

35¢
Chicago/Suburbs
50¢ Elsewhere
For home delivery
1-888-848-4637

RAIN Pages 2, 60   www.suntimes.com   WEDNESDAY, NOVEMBER 8, 2000   **Late Sports Final**

HILLARY WINS

BUSH AND GORE FIGHT THROUGH THE NIGHT IN CLOSEST
PRESIDENTIAL RACE IN 40 YEARS

Hillary Rodham Clinton celebrates her victory in the New York Senate race. It was the first time the wife of a sitting president was elected to public office. Page 6.

COVERAGE INSIDE

Dems pick up U.S. Senate seats in Florida, Delaware; Page 7
Dorothy Brown sweeps race for Cook County clerk; Page 10
Is there a ghost voter in the cardinal's residence? Page 12

Hillary turned out to be an exemplary senator. In her new position, she has incorporated an approach she used successfully in the past—building bridges that cross party lines. She works closely with Republicans, including some who were harsh critics of her husband, to promote legislation. It's not easy being a senator; in her new job Hillary works twelve- to fifteen-hour days.

True to her word, the first bill that Hillary introduced after her election was designed to provide resources to stimulate the economy in upstate New York. After the terrorist attack on the World Trade Center on September 11, 2001, she helped obtain $20 billion for the cleanup and restoration. She also authored legislation to get benefits expedited to the families of police officers, firefighters, and other public workers who died in the attacks. To make the response to emergencies such as this more effective, she introduced legislation that provides funding directly to communities according to the likelihood of threat and vulnerability to attack. She was the cosponsor of the 21st Century Nanotechnology Research and Development Act (signed into law in 2004), which is expected to create high-tech jobs in her state. She proposed job-training programs that became part of the Workforce Investment Act Amendments of 2005.

She has been a major proponent of renewal communities, economically depressed areas of the country that are targets for tax incentives to encourage business development. She was a cosponsor of the Fair Minimum Wage Act of 2005. In 2006, she authored the Heroes at Home legislation, which provides funds for mental health, readjustment, and work transition aid for members of the military returning from the war in Iraq. Along with Senator Susan Collins, Hillary authored the Positive Aging Act of 2005, designed to improve older Americans' access to mental health services. This measure was incorporated into the Older Americans Act reauthorization bill. In the wake of Hurricane Katrina, when it became apparent that the Federal Emergency Management Agency (FEMA) was not responding effectively as part of the Department of Homeland Security, Hillary introduced legislation to make FEMA once again an independent, cabinet-level federal agency.

Health care has always been important to Hillary. Some of her efforts in this area include the following: She was the main author of the Wired for Health Care Quality Act, which provides for an interactive health information and quality measurement system. She has supported the expansion of the State

Hillary attends a New Orleans press conference. Because of the poor response to Hurricane Katrina, Hillary proposed that the Federal Emergency Management Agency again be made an independent agency.

Children's Health Insurance Program, to cover parents of eligible children; the provision of tax credits to small employers who give their employees health insurance; and the providing of Medicaid coverage to the children of legal immigrants. In addition, she has succeeded in getting two amendments to the Best Pharmaceuticals for Children Act passed into law. These amendments ensure funding for the testing of children's drugs and guarantee that children have access to the most promising cancer drugs. She is the cosponsor of the Lifespan Respite

Care Act, which is designed to provide assistance to families that care for ill relatives.

The *New York Times* in an October 15, 2006, article, "The New York Senate Race," had this to say about Hillary: "Mrs. Clinton has been an excellent senator—hard-working and in close touch with her state. We have been particularly impressed by her focus on the neglected 'first suburbs' of aging housing and decaying infrastructure. As a Democrat, she has a limited ability to influence legislation, but she has taken a lead in forming the debate on a number of issues of substance. Her bill aimed at fixing the mechanics of voting set the standard for election reform legislation.

"Watching Mrs. Clinton do her job, we have been impressed by her mastery of even the most obscure details of New York's problems. Her ability to work with Republicans has been a pleasant surprise. She has won the genuine respect of most of her colleagues in Washington. . . . It seems as if in the Senate, Mrs. Clinton has found her true calling."

2006 and Beyond

In 2006, Hillary was reelected to the Senate in a landslide, receiving 70 percent of the vote. One striking aspect of her reelection campaign is how

Women in the Senate

Of the 1,884 people who have served in the Senate between 1789 and 2006, only thirty-four have been women (1.75 percent). The first woman senator was Rebecca Latimer Felton (D-Georgia), a writer and educator who served in the Senate in 1922. However, she was only appointed to fill a vacancy and served a single day. Although since 1972 there has always been a least one woman senator, as recently as 1992 there were only two women there: Nancy Kassenbaum (R-Kansas) and Barbara Mikulski (D-Maryland). One of the most well-known female senators is Margaret Chase Smith (R-Maine), who died in 1995. She holds the distinction of being the longest-serving woman senator (twenty-four years) and is in the unique position of having served in both the House of Representatives and the Senate. She was elected to the House of Representatives in 1940 and served there eight years before running for the Senate. Although in 2006 there were sixteen women senators, women are still vastly underrepresented in the Senate, given the fact that they make up more than half the population of the United States.

accepted she has become in New York, in sharp contrast to her first-term run for the Senate, when many viewed her as an outsider. She also contributed several million dollars she raised to other Democrats

Hillary is pictured here among the women senators of the 108th Congress during her first term. Fourteen of the 100 senators were women.

running in campaigns within New York and around the country.

It has long been rumored that Hillary Clinton will make a run for the White House. Her name was mentioned as a possible presidential candidate in the 2004 elections, in which George W. Bush ran for a second term. Rather than interrupt her first term as senator, she chose to wait. Hillary jumped into the 2008 presidential race on January 20, 2007, when she posted the words "I'm in" on her Web site. According to reporter Linda Feldmann of the

A victorious Hillary waves to supporters after winning reelection in 2006. She spoke of the outcome of the elections, which favored the Democratic Party, as a signal that America desired change.

Christian Science Monitor, in March 2007 Hillary and former New York mayor Rudolph Giuliani, a Republican contender for candidacy, had the greatest chance of being elected president in 2008, based on a Gallup Poll.

According to an article in the *New York Daily News,* "Easy Clinton Victory," many see Hillary as the front-running Democratic candidate. "She has put together a strong network of national advisors and donors. And she has a big lead in most early polls of Democratic primary voters. . . . 57% now say they think she could go all the way."

Will Hillary win the Democratic nomination among the crowded field of Democrats who seek the office of president? Only time will tell, but one thing is clear—if she does, she will be a formidable candidate.

October 26, 1947 Hillary Rodham is born in Chicago, Illinois.

1964 Hillary campaigns for Senator Barry Goldwater in the presidential campaign.

April 5, 1968 Martin Luther King Jr. is assassinated in Memphis.

June 5, 1968 Robert F. Kennedy is assassinated in Los Angeles.

Summer 1968 Hillary serves as a student intern in Congress.

August 26–29, 1968 A violent confrontation takes place between protesters and the Chicago police at the Democratic National Convention.

May 31, 1969 Hillary graduates from Wellesley College and gives a commencement address.

1970 Hillary meets Bill Clinton.

1973 Hillary graduates from Yale Law School.

1973 Hillary goes to work at the Children's Defense Fund.

1974 Hillary goes to work for John Doar on the impeachment of Richard M. Nixon.

October 11, 1975 Hillary marries Bill Clinton.

November 7, 1978 Bill Clinton is elected governor of Arkansas, and Hillary becomes Arkansas's First Lady.

1979 Hillary heads the Arkansas Health Advisory Committee.

February 27, 1980 Hillary gives birth to daughter Chelsea.

November 3, 1992 Bill Clinton is elected president of the United States, and Hillary becomes First Lady.

November 4, 1996 Bill Clinton is elected to a second term in the White House.

1996 Hillary writes *It Takes a Village*.

November 2001 Hillary is elected senator from New York.

November 7, 2006 Hillary is reelected to the Senate.

January 20, 2007 Hillary announces she will run for president in 2008.

GLOSSARY

apartheid The segregation of people by race or another characteristic.

Black Panthers A militant black activist organization active in the 1960s.

canvass Solicit votes or political support.

capitalism The production and sale of goods and services by individuals and companies rather than by the government.

civil rights The actions carried out mainly by African Americans and those who supported them to gain rights equal to those possessed by white people in America.

Cold War A period of intense hostility between the United States and the Soviet Union, from the end of World War II until the fall of the Soviet Union in 1991.

Communism A system of government in which all property is controlled by the state.

consternation The feeling of being confused and upset.

constituent A citizen of the locale for which an elected official is responsible.

G.I. Bill A law passed by Congress in 1944 that provides free health care, education, and other benefits to people who serve in the U.S. armed forces.

Great Depression A major economic depression that occurred in the United States in the 1930s.

impeachment The indictment of a president by the House of Representatives, for trial by the Senate. A vote of two-thirds of the senators is necessary to remove a president from office.

laudable Worthy of praise.

mammogram A type of X-ray test used to detect breast cancer.

Medicaid The government program that provides health care coverage to the poor.

Methodist A Protestant religious sect based on the beliefs of religious leader John Wesley that emphasizes personal and community morality.

menorah The eight-branched candelabra used in the celebration of Hanukkah.

micro-credit loan A small amount of money given to someone to help start a small business.

Nazi A member of the National Socialist Workers Party, which seized power in Germany in 1933 and embarked on the military conquest of Europe.

Senate Armed Services Committee A committee composed of senators that oversees issues related to the U.S. military forces.

socialism A system in which the community as a whole controls activities and property, rather than individuals.

Social Security A program instituted by the U.S. government in the 1940s that provides money to elderly and disabled people.

Watergate A Washington, D.C., apartment complex where the Democratic National Committee had its headquarters in 1972.

Weathermen A radical activist group in the 1960s that advocated the violent overthrow of the U.S. government.

FOR MORE INFORMATION

The Children's Defense Fund
25 E Street NW
Washington, DC 20001
(202) 628-8787
(800) CDF-1200 (233-1200)
Web site: http://www.childrensdefense.org

Democratic National Committee
430 S. Capitol Street SE
Washington, DC 20003
Web site: http://www.democrats.org

First Ladies National Historic Site
331 S. Market Avenue
Canton, OH 44702
(330) 452-0876
Web site: http://www.firstladies.org/index.htm

Friends of Hillary
1717 K Street NW, Suite 309A
Washington, DC 20036
Web site: http://www.hillaryclinton.com

Hillary Clinton for President
P.O. Box 2361
Chester, VA 23831
Web site: http://www.votehillary.org/CMS

Hillary Rodham Clinton Senate Office
Senator Hillary Rodham Clinton
United States Senate
476 Russell Senate Office Building
Washington, DC 20510
(202) 224-4451
Web site: http://www.clinton.
  senate.gov

HILL PAC
HILLPAC Washington Office
1717 K Street NW, Suite 309B
Washington, DC 20036
(202) 263-0190
Web site: http://www.hillpac.com

New York State Democratic Party
60 Madison Avenue
New York, NY 10010
Web site: http://www.nydems.org/
  index.asp

Web sites

Due to the changing nature of Internet links, the Rosen Publishing Group, Inc., has developed an online list of Web sites related to the subject of this book. This site is updated regularly. Please use this link to access the list:

http://www.rosenlinks.com/cp/hicl

FOR FURTHER READING

Clinton, Hillary Rodham. *Dear Socks, Dear Buddy: Children's Letters to the First Pets*. New York, NY: Simon & Schuster, 1998.

Clinton, Hillary Rodham. *An Invitation to the White House: At Home with History*. New York, NY: Simon & Schuster, 2000.

Clinton, Hillary Rodham. *It Takes a Village*. New York, NY: Simon & Schuster, 1996.

Clinton, Hillary Rodham. *Living History*. New York, NY: Scribner, 2004.

Gould, Lewis L. *American First Ladies: Their Lives and Their Legacy*. New York, NY: Routledge, 2001.

Guernsey, Joann Brenn. *Hillary Rodham Clinton*. Minneapolis, MN: First Avenue Editions, 2005.

Osborne, Claire G., ed. *The Unique Voice of Hillary Rodham Clinton*. New York, NY: Avon, 1997.

BIBLIOGRAPHY

Clinton, Bill. *My Life*. New York, NY: Random House, 2005.

Clinton, Hillary Rodham. *Living History*. New York, NY: Scribner, 2003.

Clinton, Hillary Rodham. *It Takes a Village*. New York, NY: Simon & Schuster, 1996.

Clinton, Hillary Rodham. "Wellesley College 1969 Student Commencement Speech." Retrieved October 17, 2006 (http://www.wellesley.edu/ PublicAffairs/Commencement/1969/ 053169hillary.html).

"Clinton's Quiet Path to Power." *Christian Science Monitor*. March 10, 2003. Retrieved October 19, 2006 (http://www.csmonitor.com/2003/0310/ p01s01-uspo.html).

CNN. "Hillary Rodham Clinton Scores Historic Win in New York." November 8, 2000. Retrieved October 12, 2006 (http://archives.cnn.com/2000/ ALLPOLITICS/stories/11/07/senate.ny).

Friends of Hillary. "Hillary for Senate." Press releases. Retrieved October 12, 2006 (http://www. hillaryclinton.com/press).

Marton, Kati. *Hidden Power: Presidential Marriages that Shaped Our Recent History*. New York, NY: Pantheon, 2001.

Morris, Roger. *Partners in Power: The Clintons and Their America*. New York, NY: Holt, 1996.

"The New York Senate Race." *New York Times*. October 15, 2006.

Osborne, Claire G., ed. *The Unique Voice of Hillary Rodham Clinton*, New York, NY: Avon, 1997.

INDEX

About the Author

Jeri Freedman has a B.A. from Harvard University. She is the author of a number of nonfiction books published by Rosen Publishing, as well as several plays. Under the name Ellen Foxxe, she is the coauthor of two alternate-history science fiction novels. She lives in Boston.

Photo Credits

Cover © Joshua Roberts/Getty Images; p. 5 © Matt Campbell/AFP/Getty Images; pp. 9, 40 William J. Clinton Presidential Library; pp. 13, 87 © Tim Boyle/Newsmakers/Getty Images; p. 17 © Steve Kagan/Time Life Pictures/Getty Images; pp. 20, 24 © Alan Hawes/Corbis Sygma; p. 22 © Hulton Archive/Getty Images; p. 28 © Steve Liss/Time Life Pictures/Getty Images; p. 29 © Lee Balterman/Time Life Pictures/Getty Images; p. 31 © Henry Warfield/Keystone/Getty Images; p. 35 © APA/Getty Images; p. 45 © Gene Forte/Consolidated News Pictures/Getty Images; p. 46 © Wally McNamee/Corbis; pp. 53, 54 © AP/Wide World Photos; p. 57 © Taro Yamasaki/Time Life Pictures/Getty Images; p. 60 © Joseph Sohm/ChromoSohm Inc./Corbis; p. 62 © Diana Walker/Time Life Pictures/Getty Images; p. 64 © Paul J. Richards/AFP/Getty Images; p. 66 © Brad Markel/Getty Images; p. 67 © Sharon Farmer/AFP/Getty Images; p. 73 © Sergei Guneyev/Time Life Pictures/Getty Images; p. 75 © Raveendran/AFP/Getty Images; p. 77 © The White House/AFP/Getty Images; p. 78 © MPI/Getty Images; p. 80 © Emmanuel Dunand/AFP/Getty Images; pp. 84–85 © Stephen Jaffe/AFP/Getty Images; pp. 90, 93 © Mark Wilson/Getty Images; p. 94 © Timothy A. Clary/AFP/Getty Images.

Designer: Tahara Anderson; **Editor:** Leigh Ann Cobb;
Photo Researcher: Amy Feinberg